VINCENT VAN GOGH
MASTER OF POST-IMPRESSIONIST PAINTING

JENNIFER LANDAU

Britannica®
Educational Publishing

IN ASSOCIATION WITH

ROSEN
EDUCATIONAL SERVICES

Published in 2016 by Britannica Educational Publishing (a trademark of Encyclopædia Britannica, Inc.) in association with The Rosen Publishing Group, Inc.
29 East 21st Street, New York, NY 10010

Distributed exclusively by Rosen Publishing.
To see additional Britannica Educational Publishing titles, go to rosenpublishing.com.

First Edition

Britannica Educational Publishing
J.E. Luebering: Director, Core Reference Group
Mary Rose McCudden: Editor, Britannica Student Encyclopedia

Rosen Publishing
Kathy Kuhtz Campbell: Editor
Nelson Sá: Art Director
Danijah Brevard: Designer
Cindy Reiman: Photography Manager
Karen Huang: Photo Researcher

Library of Congress Cataloging-in-Publication Data

Landau, Jennifer, 1961–
Vincent van Gogh: master of post-impressionist painting/Jennifer Landau.
    pages cm.—(Britannica beginner bios)
Includes bibliographical references and index.
ISBN 978-1-62275-946-0 (library bound)—ISBN 978-1-62275-947-7 (pbk.)—ISBN 978-1-62275-949-1 (6-pack)
1. Gogh, Vincent van, 1853-1890—Juvenile literature. 2. Painters—Netherlands—Biography—Juvenile literature. I. Title.
ND653.G7L339 2015
759.9492—dc23
[B]
                                                                                            2014039767

Manufactured in the United States of America

Photo credits: Cover, p. 15 Getty Images; p. 1, interior pages (background) Hedda Gjerpen/E+/Getty Images; pp. 4, 22 Van Gogh Museum, Amsterdam, The Netherlands/De Agostini Picture Library/Bridgeman Images; p. 5 Alinari/Getty Images; pp. 6, 26 SuperStock/Getty Images; pp. 7, 12, 17, 18, 28 De Agostini Picture Library/Getty Images; p. 8 Universal History Archive/Universal Images Group/Getty Images; p. 11 Ilberfoto/SuperStock; p. 13 National Galleries of Scotland/Hulton Fine Art Collection/Getty Images; p. 14 Dennis K. Johnson/Lonely Planet Images/Getty Images; p. 16 Rijksmuseum Kroller-Muller, Otterlo, Netherlands/Bridgeman Images; p. 19 Private Collection/Bridgeman Images; p. 20 DEA/A. Dagli Orti/De Agostini Picture Library/Getty Images; p. 21 DEA/V. Pirozzi/De Agostini Picture Library/Getty Images; p. 23 DEA/M. Carrieri/De Agostini Picture Library/Getty Images; p. 24 Peter Barritt/SuperStock/Getty Images.

CONTENTS

CHAPTER ONE

WHO WAS VINCENT VAN GOGH?

Vincent van Gogh was one of the world's most famous artists. During his lifetime, he sold only one painting. Today his paintings sell for millions of dollars.

Van Gogh lived in Europe in the 1800s. He began painting around

Self-Portrait as a Painter is one of many pictures that van Gogh painted of himself.

4

The Red Vineyard shows workers picking grapes under a bright sun.

1880. Before that, he had worked many different jobs. Van Gogh painted for just 10 years, but in those 10 years he created more than 800 paintings and 700 drawings. He moved throughout Europe during that

Quick Fact
The only painting van Gogh sold during his lifetime is titled *The Red Vineyard.*

Van Gogh painted *View of Arles with Irises* while living in Arles, France.

time, meeting many great artists along the way. In 1888, he moved to the town of Arles in France, where he did some of his best work.

As an artist, van Gogh is known for his colorful **SELF-PORTRAITS** and paintings of flowers, the countryside, and working people. He painted with great speed and deep emotion. He squeezed his tubes of oil paint directly on the canvas so that each stroke of the brush could be seen. This way of painting gave his work a unique feeling of life and movement.

Vocabulary

SELF-PORTRAITS are paintings or drawings that the artist makes of himself or herself.

Van Gogh had periods of great energy, but he also felt sad and nervous throughout his life. Even while dealing with difficult emotions, he kept painting. He is remembered as an important artist whose unusual way of painting helped change the way people look at both art and the world.

Van Gogh loved sunflowers and created many paintings of them.

CHAPTER TWO

A PAINTER'S EARLY YEARS

Van Gogh painted a Bible that had belonged to his father in *Still Life with Bible.*

Vincent Willem van Gogh was born on March 30, 1853, in Zundert, the Netherlands. He was the oldest child of Theodorus van Gogh and Anna Cornelia Carbentus. Vincent's father was a **MINISTER**. His mother studied

Vocabulary

A **MINISTER** is someone who leads the members of a church.

plants and flowers and drew many pictures of them. She thought Vincent had talent, but she did not think that he would become a great artist.

Vincent had two younger brothers named Theodorus (Theo) and Cornelius. He had three younger sisters named Anna, Elisabeth, and Willemina. He was very close to his brother Theo, who was four years younger than he was.

The van Gogh family did not have a lot of money. The eight of them lived in a very small house. The children spent many hours outside each day. Young Vincent felt a strong connection to nature and to the poor people who worked the farmland.

When Vincent was 11, he was sent to a **BOARDING SCHOOL** in another town. He felt homesick, but he did well enough in his classes to move on to another school. There he studied German, French, and English. He also took a drawing class. Within a few years, Vincent suddenly left school and returned home.

The family had to decide what their oldest son would do for a living. Three of Vincent's five uncles owned art galleries. One of these uncles was named Cent, which was short for Vincent. Uncle Cent gave Vincent a chance to learn the art business. He offered Vincent a position as an apprentice for a

Vocabulary
A **BOARDING SCHOOL** is a school where the students live instead of returning home every day.

company called Goupil. The company's main office was in Paris, France. However, Goupil also had an office in The Hague, a large city in the Netherlands. At age 16, Vincent went to work in The Hague. Later he worked for Goupil in London, from 1873 to 1875. While learning the business at Goupil, Vincent saw the work of many great artists. There were two French painters of that time that he loved: Jean-François

This is a photograph of van Gogh as a young man of 18.

Millet was a painter Van Gogh greatly admired. Here is a painting of his called *The Sower.*

Millet painted country living scenes, and Camille Corot painted landscapes.

In 1874, while working in London, Vincent became very sad. He had fallen in love with a woman who did not love him back. In 1875, he was sent to Paris, France,

Quick Fact

Between 1872 and 1890, Vincent wrote more than 600 letters to his brother Theo. He often drew pictures in his letters.

This painting is *Landscape at Coubron* by Corot, another of Van Gogh's favorite painters.

to work for Goupil, but he began to lose interest in the art business. He was mean to customers and did not always show up for work. In April 1876, he was fired from his job.

CHAPTER THREE

BECOMING AN ARTIST

Here is the home in Belgium where van Gogh lived while working as a missionary.

After he was fired from Goupil, van Gogh took other jobs. He taught at a boarding school and worked at a bookstore. He did not enjoy these jobs and decided to become a minister like his father. In 1878, van Gogh worked as a **MISSIONARY** with coal miners in Belgium. The miners were poor and had to work under

Vocabulary

A **MISSIONARY** is someone from a church who tries to spread the teachings of the church.

dangerous conditions. Van Gogh decided to give up all he owned to live more like the poor miners. He often went without food and slept on the floor. Many people thought van Gogh acted strangely. He did not get along with the people who had hired him as a missionary. They did not ask him to continue working there.

Soon van Gogh expressed an interest in creating art. In 1880, he moved to Brussels, Belgium, to study drawing. The next year, van Gogh moved to The Hague to study painting with the artist Anton Mauve. Mauve was married to van Gogh's cousin. Van Gogh set up a studio and began working with oil paints. He received support from his uncle Cornelius, who asked van Gogh to paint 12

View of the Sea at Scheveningen was stolen in 2002 and never found.

Miners' Wives Carrying Sacks of Coal shows how hard life was for poor workers.

different views of The Hague. He also received money from his brother Theo.

In 1883, van Gogh moved in with his parents in Nuenen, the Netherlands. Van Gogh did not always get along with his parents, but they let him turn the laundry room into an art studio. When his mother broke her leg, Vincent took care of her. This made Vincent's father feel better about having him in the house.

Quick Fact

While in the Netherlands, van Gogh drew many sketches of the countryside, the cottages where the farmers lived, and the tools they used to till the soil.

Van Gogh was 32 when he painted *The Potato Eaters.*

Between 1883 and 1885, Van Gogh painted nearly 200 paintings. One of these paintings was *The Potato Eaters*. The painting shows peasants sharing a meal of potatoes. Van Gogh used thick paint and dark colors in the painting. He wanted *The Potato Eaters* to look as if it had been painted with the soil of the fields in which the peasants worked. The dark colors are meant to give a feeling of how hard life was for poor people. At the time, Theo did not like his brother's painting. He said that Vincent was using darker colors than other artists and that people would not like his work. Today *The Potato Eaters* is thought of as van Gogh's first **MASTERPIECE**.

Vocabulary

A **MASTERPIECE** is an outstanding work of art.

17

CHAPTER FOUR

A NEW WAY OF PAINTING

Van Gogh's *Courtesan (after Eisen)* is modeled after Japanese prints.

Van Gogh's father died in 1885, shortly before van Gogh completed *The Potato Eaters*. Van Gogh did not stop working on his paintings. He moved to Antwerp, Belgium, later that year. He would never again return to the Netherlands. In Antwerp, he studied painting at an art school and spent time at the museums. He saw Japanese prints for the first time. He studied their simple patterns and hung many of

them on the walls where he lived.

In Antwerp, van Gogh spent what little money he had on paints and **MODELS**. He had very little left to buy food. His health was not good and he began to lose his teeth. At the art school, people laughed at the way he dressed like a workman and how his clothes were covered in paint. The instructors at the school did not like van Gogh's style of painting. Van Gogh argued with them. The instructors kept him from moving on to the next level in the school.

Van Gogh painted many pictures of people, including *Portrait of a Woman with a Red Ribbon.*

Vocabulary
MODELS are people who remain still while an artist paints them.

In 1886, van Gogh left the art school in Antwerp. He moved to Paris, France, and lived with his brother Theo. In Paris, van Gogh met artists such as Henri de Toulouse-Lautrec, Paul Signac, and Paul Gauguin. Van Gogh was very interested in a style of painting called Impressionism. In Impressionism, artists use bright colors and short strokes of the paintbrush to create scenes of daily life. Van Gogh began to use much brighter colors in his own work.

Van Gogh painted *Terrace of a Café on Montmartre (La Guinguette)* while living in Paris.

This is artist Paul Gauguin's painting called *Jokes (or Arearea)*.

Van Gogh is viewed as part of a group of artists known as Post-Impressionists. These artists did not agree on one style of painting. An artist named Georges Seurat painted by using dots of color. Paul Gauguin, who would later live with van Gogh, used bright colors to paint pictures of places such as the island of Tahiti in the South Pacific.

Quick Fact

While he lived in Paris, van Gogh painted more than 28 self-portraits.

21

CHAPTER FIVE

AN ARTIST FOR ALL TIME

Van Gogh grew tired of city life in Paris. In 1888, he moved to Arles, a town in southeastern France. Van Gogh worked long hours while in Arles. In one month alone he painted 14 pictures!

In October 1888, artist Paul Gauguin came to live with

The Yellow House is van Gogh's painting of his home in Arles.

Vase with Fifteen Sunflowers shows van Gogh's deep love of the beauty of nature.

van Gogh. To celebrate, van Gogh painted pictures of sunflowers and put them in Gauguin's room.

The two men painted together and went to visit art galleries. They fought a lot, too. Many people believe that after a bad fight between the two on Christmas Eve, 1888, van Gogh cut off the lower

Van Gogh painted *Self-Portrait with Bandaged Ear* after his fight with Gauguin.

part of his left ear. However, there are some who think that Gauguin cut off van Gogh's ear and that van Gogh said he did it himself to protect his friend. Van Gogh went to the hospital, and Gauguin moved to Paris. Shortly afterward, Van Gogh painted a self-portrait of himself with the bandaged ear.

After the fight with Gauguin, van Gogh continued to struggle with feelings of sadness and nervousness. He went to stay in a hospital in Saint-Remy to deal with his feelings. One of his most famous paintings from his year in Saint-Remy is *The Starry Night*. He painted *The Starry Night* from memory and used thick brush strokes to create the swirls of clouds in the night sky.

In 1890, van Gogh left the hospital. He moved to Auvers-sur-Oise, near Paris. One of his last paintings was *Wheat Field with Crows*, which seems to

The Starry Night is one of van Gogh's best-known paintings.

> **Quick Fact**
>
> In Arles, van Gogh lived in a house known as the Yellow House. He wanted this house to be a place where other artists would come to live and work.

match the **MOOD** that Van Gogh felt at the time. This work (pictured on page 28) shows crows in a dark sky flying above a field painted with short jabs of paint.

A few months after leaving the hospital, van Gogh became very sad and shot himself. He died two days later on July 29, 1890. Six months later, his brother Theo died from an illness. The brothers are buried next to each other in Auvers-sur-Oise, France.

> **Vocabulary**
>
> A **MOOD** is the way that you are feeling at a certain time.

Wheat Field with Crows was painted as a storm grew near.

Although van Gogh did not become famous during his lifetime, he loved to paint and showed great bravery by working even when he was ill. His paintings and drawings continue to **INSPIRE** artists all over the world.

Vocabulary

INSPIRE means to give someone an idea for what to do.

28

1853: Vincent Willem van Gogh is born on March 30 in Zundert, the Netherlands.

1864: Van Gogh is sent to boarding school in Zevenbergen, the Netherlands.

1869: Van Gogh begins working for Goupil in The Hague.

1875: Van Gogh moves to the Paris office of Goupil.

1876: Van Gogh is fired from Goupil. He moves to England to teach in a boarding school.

1877: Van Gogh returns to the Netherlands and works in a bookstore.

1878: Van Gogh works as a missionary in the Borinage, Belgium.

1879: Van Gogh is let go from his work as a missionary.

1881: Van Gogh moves to The Hague to study art with Anton Mauve.

1883: Van Gogh moves in with his parents in Nuenen, the Netherlands, and spends his days painting the countryside and the farmers' cottages and tools.

1885: Van Gogh paints *The Potato Eaters*.

1886: Van Gogh attends an art school in Antwerp, Belgium. After a short time, he moves to Paris and shares an apartment with his brother Theo.

1888: Van Gogh moves to Arles, France. He paints *The Café Terrace on the Place du Forum, Arles, at Night* and many other paintings. Paul Gauguin moves in with van Gogh, but the two argue often. Van Gogh loses part of his left ear after a fight with Gauguin.

1889: Van Gogh is hospitalized in Saint-Rémy-de-Provence. While he is there, he paints *The Starry Night*, one of his most famous paintings.

1890: Van Gogh's *The Red Vineyard* sells for 400 Belgian francs. He moves to Auvers-sur-Oise, France, where he takes his own life at the age of 37.

GLOSSARY

DANGEROUS Harmful.

EMOTION A strong feeling.

FAMOUS Known by many.

GALLERIES Rooms or buildings used to show and sell works of art.

HOMESICK Missing your home and family when away from them.

MUSEUMS Buildings where great works of art are shown.

PEASANTS Poor farmers.

STUDIO A room or place where an artist works.

STYLE The way something is made or shown.

FOR MORE INFORMATION

BOOKS

Anholt, Laurence. *Van Gogh and the Sunflowers.* Hauppauge, NY: Barron's Educational Series, 2007.

Sabbeth, Carol. *Van Gogh and the Post-Impressionists for Kids.* Chicago, IL: Chicago Review Press, 2011.

Wood, Alix. *Vincent van Gogh.* New York, NY: Windmill Books, 2013.

WEBSITES

Because of the changing nature of Internet links, Rosen Publishing has developed an online list of websites related to the subject of this book. This site is updated regularly. Please use this link to access this list:

http://www.rosenlinks.com/BBB/Gogh

INDEX